It's Career Day

by Natalie Jackson
Illustrated by Beatriz Mello

ISBN: 978-1-7386499-0-7 (Paperback)
ISBN: 978-1-7386499-2-1 (Paperback)

ISBN: 978-1-7386499-1-4 (Hardcover)

Any references to historical events, real people, or real places are used fictitiously. Names, characters, and places are products of the author's imagination.

Book Cover by Beatriz Mello.
Illustrated by Beatriz Mello.

First printing edition 2023.

Dear readers,
You will figure it out. Some people might change their career path more than once until they actually choose their dream job. Life is about building dreams for the future.

Keep dreaming! It's never late to discover your dreams. Happy career day! I dedicate this book to my grandparents.Thank you for believing me every step of the way. This book is for you with love.

Hi! I'm Gabriella. In class today, my teacher Mrs. Walker said we are going to have career day tomorrow. She has been planning this for months.

"If you look really close on the calendar, you'll see career day underlined in red marker."

Mrs. Walker looked towards the class and said, "can anyone tell me what is career day? The classroom suddenly got really silent. Gabriella's hand went up, and she said, "career day is having a job, like you do, Mrs. Walker!"

"You're right, Gabriella," said Mrs. Walker. "It gives you a chance to think about what jobs you want in the future, and to learn about these jobs. Tomorrow our class is going to have a visit from a variety of guest speakers. Make sure you ask many questions because it gives you ideas of what you want to be when you grow up," said Mrs. Walker.

"You already know my job. As your teacher, I teach you how to write and read."

Gabriella was glad that she would be able to discover her future career alongside her classmates and best friends Emmett and Brenda. She moved her chair over to Emmett and Brenda's desk and whispered, "I bet we'll see a firefighter. I'm sure we'll see a doctor, maybe even a professional dancer, or an actor."

Emmett and Brenda nodded their head while concentrating on their classwork. They both replied, "we'll just have to wait and see tomorrow."

The next day in class was the big day of career day. The students took their seats quietly, patiently waiting on the arrival of the guest speakers, but all of a sudden there was a knock at the door. Mrs. Walker opened the door, and in walked a firefighter, a doctor, a professional dancer and actor just as Gabriella said.

Emmett, Brenda and Gabriella looked at each other surprised and started to giggle. No later than two minutes, there was another knock at the door this time louder and in entered a lawyer, a chef, a pilot, a hairdresser, a dentist, a veterinarian, a painter, a secretary, a nurse, an optometrist and a realtor.

"Wow! It's really getting very crowded in here." Mrs. Walker said.

The firefighter introduced himself to the class first and said, “I’m a trained firefighter. I work to put out fires, and evacuate people and animals to safety. A firefighter wears a special uniform to keep them safe from smoke and heat. I help with medical emergencies, that means I help anyone who needs help because they’re hurt, and I’m the first one on the scene.”

“Do you need to be very strong to be a firefighter?” Asked Gabriella.

“Yes, it’s important to be strong enough so you can carry all your equipment, such as your ladder and fire hose, and strong enough to carry a person to safety from the fire,” said the firefighter.

The students were all led outside to see the fire truck.

Next the doctor introduced herself to the class. She said, "I'm a doctor, there are many types of doctors specialized in different medical areas. A doctor works with nurses, doctors and other hospital staff. I help to make sick people feel better. When they come see me, I identify what is causing them to be sick and I treat them to get better. As a trained doctor, I prescribe medicine, I send people to a specialist if they need one. That means a person that is trained to take care of that certain problem. I help people to stay healthy by getting checkups."

“Why do doctors use stethoscopes?” Asked Emmett.

“To check a person’s heart and lungs, by listening through a stethoscope we can make sure they’re healthy,” said the doctor.

The doctor brought her stethoscope and let the students pass it around the class.

Next the professional dancer introduced himself to the class. He said, "I'm a dancer, I can work in dance schools, in television, concerts or theatres. I learn complex dance moves and many different styles of dance such as ballet, tap, hip-hop, jazz and contemporary. I tell a story through dance to connect to the audience. Some dancers are self-employed. That means they find their own work, or are represented by an agency. That's when someone else finds work for you.
A dancer has to practice everyday and is constantly learning new dances."

"Do you ever forget your dance moves on stage?" Asked Brenda.

"Yes, sometimes I forget my dance moves on stage, but as a dancer I learnt to not panic and just keep dancing." Said the professional dancer. "Find a space on the floor and I'll show you guys some Hip-hop and Tap moves."

The students all found a spot on the floor and tried to copy the dance moves.

Next the actor introduced herself to the class. She said, “I’m an actor, I perform in television, commercials and in movies, sometimes as an extra and sometimes as a lead actor. Extra means you have no speaking lines, the lead actor is someone with bigger lines. I get my work by doing auditions. This means you perform your act in front of people who are searching for talents. If you’re good you get the job. As an actor I also memorize my lines and rehearse them, that means to practise them over and over.”

“Do you get nervous before each audition?” Asked Gabriella.
“Yes, I do get nervous before auditions, and I remain calm by listening to music that helps me relax before entering any auditions.” Said the actor.

The actor gave each student a small line to see how well their acting skills were. She was quite impressed how fast the students picked up and how brilliant they were.

Next the lawyer introduced himself. He said, "I'm a lawyer. Another name for lawyer is attorney. There are different types of lawyers that work with different situations depending on a person's needs. I am trained in law that means rules. Laws are something we all follow to keep us safe and keep other people safe as well. I give my advice to people about following the rules. I defend people in court by arguing a client's case to protect a person's rights. As a lawyer, you have to love reading and writing because it's part of what lawyers do."

"What is one thing you don't like about your job?" Asked Emmet.

"One thing I don't like about my job is the long hours, as a lawyer I work for a long period of time catching up with work." Said the Lawyer.

The lawyer gave each student a pen with their names, and said, "you will have to write a lot if you become a lawyer."

Next the chef introduced herself. She said, "I'm a chef. I help supervise a team of cooks, and manage the kitchen, that means I make sure everything goes well in the kitchen. I can work in a restaurant, school or hotel. I make sure the food looks and tastes good and I create what goes on the menu and price them as well. As a chef, I'm busy with handling more than one task at a time in the kitchen."

“Why did you choose to be a chef?” Asked Brenda.

“I love being a chef because I love cooking and getting creative with the food presentation. That means how nice the food looks on the plate, because food doesn’t just have to taste good but look good as well.”

The chef showed pictures of her own cookbook and let the students pass it around.

Next the pilot introduced himself to the class. He said, “I’m a pilot, I fly airplanes and other aircrafts. My job is to carry people from one place to another. I have to think quickly on what decisions to make if faced with weather conditions or emergencies. I make sure my manual is up to date, that means the instructions book for the plane. I make sure all is updated if there are new changes. I do a routine check before the plane takes off. I check for the tires, make sure there are no leaks, the lights work and engine fan blades are in good condition.”

“What do the stripes on the pilot’s uniform mean?” Asked one of the students.

"The stripes mean what level you are at from beginner to advanced. The stripes on your shoulder are called epaulets, then you also got stripes on your sleeves. One stripe means that you're in training, two stripes mean second officer and in training. The third stripe is when a pilot is first officer, four stripes mean that person is the captain and in charge. The captain usually sits on the left side in an airplane." Said the pilot.

The pilot gave each student their own pilot wings pin and said, "these wings will motivate you to get your real ones someday if you ever want to become a pilot."

Next the hairdresser introduced herself to the class. She said, "I am a hairdresser. I cut, shampoo, colour hair, and style. When someone visits my salon they tell me what style they want and I help to give them ideas if they are not sure what they want. I show them how to take care of their hairdo at home. I'm always learning new hair styles, because it's always changing. I clean my work area and tools before taking the next person and I book hair appointments."

“Have you ever had a customer who didn’t like their hair style?” Asked Gabriella.

“Yes, we do have customers who do not like their hair style. I fix the problem right away so they are happy customers.” Said the hairdresser.

The hairdresser showed some hairstyles of her most popular hairdos to the students.

Next the dentist introduced himself. He said, "I'm a dentist. I make sure your teeth are healthy and clean by brushing and flossing the right amount of time that is needed. I do checkups to make sure there are no cavities by taking pictures of your mouth, which is called an Xray. I do dental cleaning to remove food that you can't remove with a toothbrush, which is called tartar. I also repair any broken tooth that is cracked or broken."

“How often should I get a dental checkup?” Asked Emmet.

“You should get a dental checkup at least every six months even if you don’t have any problem with your teeth. It all depends on how well you take care of your teeth and your dentist will decide how many visits you need.” Said the dentist.

The dentist gave the students each a bag with toothbrush, toothpaste and floss to keep their teeth healthy.

Next the veterinarian introduced herself to the class. She said, "I am a veterinarian. That means I am a doctor for animals. There are different kinds of veterinarians, some work with only dogs and cats and others work with exotic animals. That means animals that are rare and you usually don't own as pets. I do checkups for animals to make sure they are in good health. I take care of sick and hurt animals, sometimes an animal may need a needle if they are sick or just to keep them healthy. If an animal has a wound, that means any cut, burn or injury, I would clean and bandage it. I check the animal's teeth and gums to make sure they're healthy and do Xrays and surgeries. I also teach people how to take care of their pets at home."

“What advice would you give someone who wants to become a veterinarian?” Asked Brenda.

“Taking care of your own pets can help you learn to care for animals. Reading books about animals, volunteering at a shelter, and watching tv shows about animals are all ways that can help you learn about animals.” Said the veterinarian.

The veterinarian brought in a few animals to show the students how to properly take care of them.

Next the painter introduced himself to the class. He said, "I am a painter, my job allows me to paint outdoors and indoors. Before I start painting, I cover the floors and the furniture so paint will not mess up the surface. I decide what is the best paint brush to use for the job, depending on the type of paint being used. I remove any doorknobs and light switch covers before starting. Then I start removing any old paints on the area I'm painting by scraping and sandpapering. I mix the paint really well before I begin to use it."

"What is the most difficult part of your job?" Asked Gabriella.

"The most difficult part of my job would be meeting quick deadlines, and working in different weather conditions such as hot temperature." Said the painter.

The painter handed out some paint brushes and paint to the students to inspire them to be creative with paint.

Next the secretary introduced herself. She said, "I am a secretary. I can work in an office, school, or hospital. My job is to answer phone calls, transfer the calls to the right person, check voicemail that are left on the phone. I make sure client and employee files are up to date. I confirm customers' appointments, greet customers and visitors as they arrive, and direct them to the right place or to the right person. I also set up meetings and type letters. I order office supplies that are needed for the office."

“What’s your favorite thing about the job?” Asked Emmet.

“My favorite thing about my job is working with my coworkers because they are super nice. I also get to decorate my own office space.” Said the secretary.

The secretary passed some notebooks and sticky notes to each student to help them to stay organized with taking notes in class.

Next the nurse introduced himself. He said, "I'm a nurse. I could work in a clinic, nursing home, school or a hospital. There are many different types of nurses, and they can specialize working as a pediatric nurse. That's working with children. There's a labour and delivery nurse,which takes care of mother and baby. Geriatric nurse is a nurse who takes care of elderly patients. As a nurse I check on my patient's vital signs. That means I check your blood pressure with my blood pressure cuff, it wraps around a patient's upper arm that lets me know if your blood pressure is high or low.

I take your temperature by using a thermometer, it lets me know if you have a fever. I check the patient's pulse by putting two fingers on their wrist, which allows me to feel their heart rate. I check your oxygen with my oximeter to see if your oxygen level is too low by placing a clip on your finger. I give medicine and teach patients how to take care of their injury or illness."

“What classes help you prepare for becoming a nurse?” Asked Brenda.

“Chemistry, English, Biology, Science, Math, Statistics and Physics are a few of the classes needed.” Said the nurse.

Next the optometrist introduced herself to the class. She said, “I’m an optometrist, which means an eye doctor. I take care of people’s eyes, keeping their vision sharp and healthy. I examine people’s eyes to make sure they don’t have any diseases that can affect your vision. I test people’s vision by letting them read a bunch of letters to see if their vision is clear or blurry by covering one eye at a time. I use a machine called phoropter. This machine allows me to see what letters you see better through many different lenses. If you see blurry, I check if you need glasses for farsightedness or nearsightedness.

That means you can see things far much better than things near or that you can see things near better than things far away.”

“What other job would you choose if you didn’t do what you do now?” Asked one of the students.

“The job that I would choose if I didn’t do what I do now, would be working as a construction worker. They tear down buildings, rebuild new buildings and build highways and roads.” Said the optometrist.

The optometrist handed out her business card to the students to bring home if they ever needed glasses.

Next the realtor introduced himself. He said, "I'm a realtor, my job is to help people buy or sell homes. I help people find the type of home they're looking for by listening to their needs. Some people might want a big home or small home, some people might want a backyard or a home with not too many stairs. I take all the information they are looking for and help them find their perfect home. I help people sell their home by preparing it for sale. I will help them price their home and fix things in each room to make it look nicer and brighter which is called "staging" then I will take photos and help them sell their home."

“What is a normal day as a realtor like?” Asked Gabriella.

“A normal day as a realtor would be just meeting with people, showing homes and being in the office checking emails and taking or returning phone calls.” Said the realtor.

The realtor played a game with the students to find out if they know what kind of homes match to what the person is saying they’re looking for.

As soon as the last guest speaker finished speaking to the class, they all waved goodbye and exited out in the same order they came in: the firefighter, the doctor, the professional dancer, the actor, the lawyer, the chef, the pilot, the hairdresser, the dentist, the veterinarian, the painter, the secretary, the nurse, the optometrist and the realtor.

The students all waved goodbye and then Mrs. Walker approached the class and said, "wasn't it fantastic hearing about the jobs people do? I am going to pass a paper on each of your desks and I would like you to write your name and the job that interests you the most, and why you want to be that when you grow up."

Emmet scribbled on his paper with no hesitation and wrote what he wanted to be when he grows up. Brenda completed her paper slightly slower and pushed her paper at the end of her desk. The rest of the class were all done writing on their papers.

Gabriella was still thinking what she wanted to be, she had no idea, even though there were a lot of guest speakers whose jobs sounded amazing.

Mrs. Walker walked in each aisle of the classroom and picked up each student's paper and put it in her folder. When she got to Gabriella's desk, she noticed a blank paper with nothing written down.

When Mrs. Walker asked Gabriella, "do you need more time to think about what you want to be when you grow up?" Gabriella said, "yes Mrs. Walker." Mrs. Walker handed back Gabriella's paper and told her that she could take her paper home and bring it back tomorrow morning.

When Gabriella arrived at home she greeted her mom in the kitchen and said, "mom, in school we had career day, but I didn't complete the paper Mrs. Walker handed out in class, so she allowed me to bring it home. I didn't know what I want to be when I grow up."

"You will figure it out, don't worry, everyone doesn't know exactly what they want to be at the same time. Just think back on the career day you had in school. Do you like working with animals or people? What kind of things do you enjoy doing?" Gabriella's mom said.

Gabriella went to her room, got out some other pieces of paper, and started to write down ideas of what she wanted to be when she grows up. She threw paper after paper in the garbage until it looked almost like a pyramid.

After scribbling and erasing and throwing out papers, she realized what she wanted to be. Gabriella took out the paper from Mrs. Walker and wrote her name and what she wanted to be when she grows up. She then folded her paper and put it inside her school bag.

Next morning in class Gabriella took her seat near her two best friends Emmett and Brenda. Mrs. Walker said, “I will be reading out everyone’s papers I picked up yesterday for career day, about what you want to be when you grow up.” She started to read everyone’s papers. Some of them wanted to be dentists, lawyers, chefs, painters, and firefighters.

When Mrs. Walker got to Emmett's paper it said he wanted to be a pilot because he likes planes and it would be cool to learn to drive one when he gets older and go to pilot school.

When Mrs. Walker read Brenda's paper, she said she wanted to be a veterinarian because she loves taking care of animals.

“There is one paper missing.” Mrs. Walker said and Gabriella replied, “that would be my paper, Mrs. Walker.” Gabriella went to the front of the class and handed her paper to Mrs. Walker and went back to her desk.

She started reading Gabriella's paper and it said, "when I grow up, I want to be an actor because I like to be on television someday in one of my favorite shows. I also want to be a professional dancer because I love music and dancing and someday, I want to perform in a huge concert. I also want to be a realtor because I like helping people find the homes of their dreams and I have good listening skills."

After a long time being undecided of what she wanted to be when she grows up, Gabriella realized she couldn't just choose one career, because her dreams included all three.

SALE

About The Author

Natalie Jackson is a dancer, actor and author. She has been dreaming about crafting stories ever since she was old enough to read. It's Career Day is the first book born out of her passion to write. When she is not writing you can find her enjoying a good book with a cup of hot chocolate.

www.ingramcontent.com/pod-product-compliance
Lightning Source LLC
Chambersburg PA
CBHW041921180726
48295CB00002B/29

* 9 7 8 1 7 3 8 6 4 9 9 0 7 *